GEEN PARTIJ

I WUZ BAD

I HIDE NOW

PUSSYCAT

CAN'T POOP WHEN U WATCH

‘SUP BRO

I CAN HAS CHEEZBURGER?

I CAN HAS HUGGLE?

THIS IS SERIUS BIZNIS

I'M IN UR WIKI
RVRTIN UR EDITS

JAZZ HANDS!

LOL

IM IN UR FOLDER

KERUPTIN UR FYLEZ

UNINTERESTED CAT
IS UNINTERESTED

BUSTED

MUST...ACT...ADORABLE

YOU MAKE LOL CAT CRY!!!!

I HELP WIF UR SHOPPING

OH HI
I COME FROM
INTERNET

I SEE WHAT U DID THERE

IM IN UR BED
ZLEEPING

WWW.GEENPARTIJ.NL

DESIGNED IN AMSTERDAM

www.ingramcontent.com/pod-product-compliance
Lightning Source LLC
Chambersburg PA
CBHW081803280526
45789CB00008B/2974
* 9 7 8 1 5 3 9 9 6 9 5 4 9 *